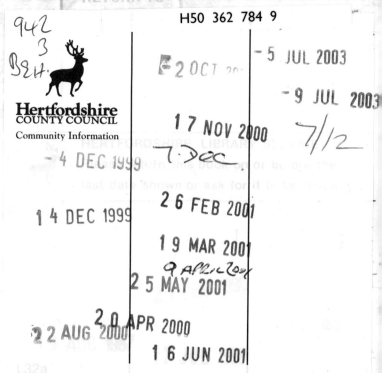

D1587506

WESTCOUNTRY SHIPWRECKS

A Pictorial Record 1866-1973

The *Rosedale* wrecked on Porthminster beach, St Ives.
November 1893

WESTCOUNTRY SHIPWRECKS

A Pictorial Record
1866-1973

JOHN BEHENNA

DAVID & CHARLES

NEWTON ABBOT LONDON NORTH POMFRET (VT)
VANCOUVER

To my Father,
JOSHUA BEHENNA,
and
in memory of
UNCLE NAT

ISBN 0 7153 6569 X

Set in 11 on 13pt Imprint and printed in
Great Britain by Compton Printing Limited, Aylesbury
for David & Charles (Holdings) Limited
South Devon House, Newton Abbot, Devon

Published in the United States of America
by David & Charles Inc, North Pomfret
Vermont 05053, USA

Published in Canada by Douglas, David &
Charles Limited, 3645 McKechnie Drive
West Vancouver, BC

CONTENTS

INTRODUCTION

On a fine summer's day at dead low water on a spring tide, a keen-eyed visitor tramping around any part of the coast of the Westcountry would not have to walk far before spotting an incongruous shape among the rocks below the cliffs or lying partly covered by sand on a beach or in a cove. It will probably be the remains of one of the countless shipwrecks that have occurred around these coasts over the centuries, some recent, but many long forgotten.

Among the many examples that come readily to mind are the bottom plates of the steamer *Collier* wrecked in Rockham Bay in 1914, the propeller-shaft of the steamer *Welbury* lying under Longpeak since 1882, the bottom timbers of the brig *Albert Wilhelm* uncovered on Lelant beach in 1968 after lying there since 1886, the seaweed-covered boilers of the *City of Cardiff* blown ashore in Nanjizal Bay in 1912, the boiler of the steamer *Jane Rowe* lost under Bolberry Down in 1914 and the bow of the 'onion wreck' *Louise Yvonne* wedged under Prawle Point, where she ran aground in fog in 1935. In some cases it is only the cargo that remains, like the 800 tons of rock-hard bags of cement thrown overboard to lighten the coaster *Olivine* when she went ashore in Horseley Cove in 1929.

Since the early 1860s many of these wrecks have been recorded by the camera and this book brings together a selection from my own collection of photographs of Westcountry shipwrecks, many of which are of particular interest to the shipping historian as the only pictorial record in existence of certain of the ships. Some evoke memories of the serenity and quietness of times now past, whilst others, by their contrast with the contemporary scene, are a valuable record of the unspoilt coastline before much ugly development took place.

My interest in shipwrecks was probably to be expected, since I was born into a seafaring family at St Ives, where conversation was never very far away from ships in general and wrecks in particular. My grandfather, then serving as a cabin boy, was picked up from the sea, clinging to a hatch, when the brigantine *Eliza* sank near Lundy on 27 March 1873. My father was shipwrecked in World War I, and in 1917 had a narrow escape off the Cornish coast when a torpedo passed under his ship, Hain's *Trelawney*, and exploded on the rocks below Cape Cornwall. After leaving the sea, he joined the St Ives LSA Brigade, serving for eighteen years, for six of which he was also an auxiliary coastguard. My great-uncle Nathaniel, who lived with us, was also a member of the LSA for over twenty years, receiving a long-service medal on 3 October 1925, and was also the Shipwrecked Mariners Society's representative at St Ives from 1916 to 1932, taking care of many survivors from local shipwrecks. Among his prized possessions, and in front of me as I write, was a letter from the secretary of the Society thanking him for looking after the crew of the *Lyminge*, wrecked at Gurnards Head in September 1931. He had a great love of ships and was probably the only postman who carried a three-foot long telescope in his postbag in case he spotted something interesting out at sea.

Although he walked over ten miles every day collecting and delivering mail to the many scattered farmhouses between St Ives and Zennor, at lunchtime he would walk an extra mile to Zennor headland so that he could 'spy' out the shipping passing up and down the coast while he ate his pasty. As a young boy, he used to thrill me with daring tales of wreck work. His first rescue was at the wreck of the ship *Alexander Yeats* on Gurnards Head in September 1896, when he helped carry the rocket apparatus five miles along the coast to rescue the crew of nineteen. By coincidence, fifty-eight years later on 25 July 1954, the German coaster *Traute Sarnow* was wrecked at almost the same spot. It was my father's last rescue and I vividly remember driving with him through dense fog along the twisting coastal road and drinking rum at 3 am in the local inn after the crew had been got safely ashore.

Uncle Nathaniel, known affectionately in St Ives as Nat, had a small collection of about twenty shipwreck photographs which he bequeathed to me when he died in 1951. I have been adding steadily to these ever since and today the collection comprises over 2,000 photographs. These have come from many sources, including museums, long-standing photographic businesses such as that of Gibson in the Scilly Isles, junk and antique shops, fellow shipwreck enthusiasts, jumble sales and family photograph albums. One rare wreck photograph was found on a corporation refuse dump, a sad reminder that much valuable material is lost for ever when perhaps a loft is cleared of its 'junk', or the personal effects of a deceased person are thrown away by unsuspecting relatives.

I have also photographed many of the latter-day shipwrecks using a 35 mm ILOCA f/2·8 camera. This has often entailed a quick dash by car followed by a scramble across fields and clifftop to photograph a casualty before she broke up. Some of these excursions have not been without incident, such as when a winch being used for salvage work on the coaster *Alacrity* at Portheras Cove in 1963 toppled over the cliff edge, narrowly missing my wife who had started climbing the cliff ahead of me. On another occasion, in March 1969, an enforced stay part way up the 500 ft Sandor Cliffs after climbing down to photograph the wreck of the French trawler *Goliath* was a warning that sometimes it is easier to clamber down than to climb up a cliff.

A great deal of detective work is sometimes involved in the identification of an unnamed wreck photograph. The general outline of the wrecked ship itself, or maybe the dress of the people in the picture, can often provide an approximate date of a wreck. By comparing other features with details from newspaper files, the choice can be narrowed still further and perhaps a final clue may be provided by establishing the name of the owners of a particular wreck and then comparing the funnel markings of that company with those in the photograph. On occasions, final identification has been made by reading about the position of a wreck and then walking along the coast to that particular spot to compare the coastline with that in the photograph. It can be very gratifying to walk around a headland and see the view in the photograph unfold itself.

A reader who is tempted to collect Westcountry wreck photos, could not do better than start with the magnificent collection taken by the Gibson family of the Scilly Isles, who have been photographing wrecks since the early 1870s.

In choosing the photographs for this book, I have endeavoured to arrive at a selection that would cover the region geographically and at the same time would be representative of the period from the 1860s until the present day. Unfortunately, this means that some well-known local wrecks have had to be omitted, but it is hoped that the photographs selected will adequately portray an important and interesting aspect of the local history of a region where the sea plays a very large part in the way of life of its people.

JOHN BEHENNA

Galmpton, Devon

1 NINETEENTH-CENTURY SHIPWRECKS

WILD ROSE

The camera has recorded the dramatic scene at Brixham after the great hurricane of 10–11 January 1866, when over forty ships were driven ashore or foundered in Torbay. The least damaged ship among the splintered remains of the eight ships which piled up against the New Pier is the barque *Wild Rose* of Whitby. Bound from Odessa for Dublin with a cargo of wheat, she had been among the ninety-four ships sheltering in Torbay from a sw gale when the wind suddenly backed to the NE and increased to hurricane force. All the crew of eleven of the *Wild Rose* were hauled to safety by local men clinging to ropes and nets slung over the pier, but over 100 lives were lost in the other wrecks.

It is interesting to note the fields in the background which, today, are completely built over with houses, hotels and flats. The barque in line with the end of the pier is the *Princess Beatrice* of Sunderland, which was later refloated. Behind her a ship can be seen on the stocks in one of Brixham's then thriving shipbuilding yards.

GANNET

A photographer from St Ives probably walked miles to take this unique photograph of the three-masted schooner-rigged steamer *Gannet* of Cork, wrecked under Morvah Cliffs, about one mile east of Pendeen Watch. She ran into the cliffs in clear weather just before midnight on 26 May 1871 'with the ship under fore and aft sails with about 8 lbs steam going about 8 knots', to quote her captain's official report. The crew, the stewardess, a lady passenger and her child all took to the boats and rowed to St Ives, arriving there at 5 o'clock next morning. The *Gannet* was bound from Liverpool for Antwerp with a cargo of rock salt, cotton wool, palm oil and mahogany. She broke up, but much of her cargo was salvaged by Harveys of Hayle.

The *Gannet*, of 817 tons gross, was owned by E. Pyke of Cork, and had been built in 1867.

The sea is now in a peaceful mood at Bigbury Bay, but the wrecked barque bears witness to the severe SSW gale that had recently swept over the area. The victim was the *Lady Young* of Liverpool, built of wood at Quebec in 1870 with a registered tonnage of 589. She was driven ashore in the gale at Westdown Point, near Bantham, just before midnight on 20 October 1879 whilst bound from Hamburg for Cardiff in ballast. Hope Cove coastguards observed her distress signals before she struck and the crew of thirteen were safely taken off by breeches buoy. However, next day the steward, returning to the wreck to collect some of his belongings, fell out of the bosun's chair onto the rocks 50 ft below and was killed. The barque herself went to pieces in renewed gales a few days later. In the background of the photo is Burgh Island, which today is dominated by a large hotel.

BALBEC

A heavy ground swell sweeps into Nanjizal Bay, a mile SE of Land's End, where the Cunard liner *Balbec* lies a total wreck. Behind her, the majestic cliffs of Carn Les Boel, Carn Barra and Carn Guthenbras stretch into the distance, while the Diamond Horse Rock dominates the foreground. The *Balbec's* captain ran her aground on 28 March 1884, after she had struck a submerged object near the Longships and started to fill with water. She was on passage from Liverpool to Le Havre with a general cargo, and her crew of twenty-nine, together with five passengers, landed safely from the ship's own boats.

Registered at Glasgow, the *Balbec* was built at Dumbarton in 1853. Her gross tonnage was 774, and she was 209·2 ft in length, with a beam of 30·3 ft.

The Sunderland-registered steamer *Avebury* lies wrecked with her bow high up on the rocks under Rosemodress Cliff, about half a mile south-west of Lamorna Cove, where she ran aground in thick fog on 28 October 1884. On passage from Lisbon to Cardiff with a cargo of iron ore and esparto grass, she had taken a course too far to the eastwards when attempting to round the Land's End in the fog. Her crew of sixteen were brought safely ashore by breeches buoy, but the ship became a total loss. The tattered sail on her foremast is a reminder that those early steamers still took advantage of wind as well as engine power.

The *Avebury*, owned by John Chapman, was built at Middlesborough in 1870 with a gross tonnage of 738, a length of 200 ft, and with engines of 99 hp.

Early on the morning of 8 June 1885 the three-masted schooner-rigged steamer *Earl of Lonsdale,* registered at Newcastle, was steaming – contrary to all rules for safe navigation – at full speed in a dense fog. Her estimated position was ten miles south of the Bishop but, in fact, she was heading for disaster as the Rennell current had carried her to the northwards, and at 3 am she crashed onto rocks off St Agnes, near Troy Town in the Isles of Scilly. She was carrying a cargo of cotton from Alexandria to Portishead, and was manned by a crew of twenty-two, all of whom were saved. The severe impact ripped several holes in her bottom and she had to be abandoned as a total loss. The photograph was taken a few days later, after the top of her mizzen mast had been broken off and her fore and main masts had suffered damage due to the pounding on the rocks from a swell sweeping up the narrow channel between St Agnes and Annet.

Built of iron at North Shields in 1872, the *Earl of Lonsdale* had a gross tonnage of 1,543 and her engines developed 140 hp. Her dimensions were: length 247 ft 8 in, breadth 33 ft 6in, and depth of hold 23 ft 2in. She was owned by George G. Dunford of Newcastle.

NEWTON

A high spring tide has carried the West Hartlepool steamer *Newton* right up under the foot of the cliffs at Higher Sharpnose Point, not far from where the Rev R. S. Hawker, the poet-vicar of Moorwenstow, built his little hut from which he kept a lookout for ships in distress. The *Newton,* launched by Swan Hunter at Newcastle in 1883, was wrecked in thick fog on 21 March 1886 while on passage from Bremerhaven to Newport in ballast. The crew of eighteen fixed a spar from the bows on to the rocks and climbed safely ashore. The wrecked ship was later sold for £30.

Owned by Hardy Wilson & Co, the *Newton* was 1,423 tons gross, with a length of 245·5 ft and a breadth of 34·2 ft. Her engines developed 123 hp.

The three-masted schooner-rigged steamer *Suffolk* lies with her back broken directly under Lizard Head, which she hit at speed in dense fog during the afternoon of 28 September 1886. Her mainmast, funnel and midship-structure have disappeared, and the solitary bullock standing on her forecastle head appears to be the only one remaining from the 161 which had been taken aboard at Baltimore, for London. Many were washed overboard from the decks on which they had been penned, and drowned, but about fifty were hauled up the cliffs to safety. The forty-three crew and two passengers were rescued by the Lizard and Cadgwith lifeboats after they had taken to the ship's boats.

The *Suffolk*, registered at London, was built at Blackwall in 1881 by R. & H. Green for the Atlantic Transport Line. She had a gross tonnage of 2,924, a length of 300 ft, a beam of 40·25 ft, and a depth of 22·25 ft.

MARIE EMELIE

Crowds of onlookers have gathered on Ilfracombe pierhead to watch salvage operations being carried out on the Barnstaple-registered ketch *Marie Emelie*. Bound from Newport to her home port with a cargo of coal, she went onto the rocks on 18 October 1886 in moderate ENE winds. Her crew of two were saved but the ketch, after refloating, was found to be damaged beyond repair and was broken up at Ilfracombe. Of 37 tons register, the French-built *Marie Emelie* had been bought by A. Gerrard of Barnstaple shortly before her loss. The prominent 450 ft high cliffs of Hillsborough sloping down to Beacon Point can be seen behind the pier.

MALTA

Half a mile to the north-east of Cape Cornwall lies the headland known as Kenidjack Castle, and it was here, during a dense fog, that the Cunard liner *Malta* of Glasgow ran aground on 15 October 1889. She was bound from Liverpool to Genoa with nineteen passengers and a general cargo. All passengers and crew were saved, most of them getting ashore in the ship's boats. The *Malta*, of 2,244 gross tonnage and built by J. & G. Thomson at Glasgow in 1865, became a total wreck, the second Cunarder to be lost on the Cornish coast within five years. The small boats in the photograph belong to local miners and fishermen and are keeping close to the doomed ship as her valuable cargo, including bottles of wine and beer, kegs of spirits, velveteen, rugs and carpets, floats to the surface from her broken holds.

(facing page, below)

Projecting into the sea, the headland of Pendeen Watch became a veritable grave-yard of ships before the present lighthouse was completed there in 1900. One of its victims, the Cardiff-registered steamer *Scheldt*, wrecked during dense fog on 23 June 1890, lies between the Three Stone Oar rocks and the cliffs. She was on passage from Newport to Bordeaux with a cargo of coal. The crew of seventeen landed safely in nearby Portheras Cove in their own boats.

At a subsequent Board of Trade enquiry, the captain had his master's certificate suspended for six months after being found guilty of failing to verify his course on nearing Land's End and failing to use the lead. The *Scheldt*, owned by the Cardiff Steamship Co, had a gross tonnage of 1,090 and was built at Bristol in 1884.

KISHON

Most of the sailing ships wrecked at Bude were coastal ketches and schooners, but on 7 November 1890 a deep-sea sailing ship stranded on the western end of Bude breakwater during a NW gale. She was the British barque *Kishon* of North Shields, which had earlier broken away from the tug *Australia* while being towed from London to Appledore in ballast. The Bude LSA fired a line over the stranded ship and pulled the crew ashore to safety in the breeches buoy over massive breakers which were thundering down on the rocks around the stranded ship. The *Kishon*, built at Hylton in 1872 by J. Gardener, broke up on the next tide. She was 143 ft long, with a beam of 29 ft and a registered tonnage of 491.

MARIA

In the thick fog that enveloped the South Devon coast on the morning of 27 June 1892, the Greek steamship *Maria*, of Andros, ran onto the Langler Rocks on the western side of Prawle Point, the tide being full at the time. She was miles off course, being bound to Rotterdam with a cargo of wheat and barley. In this illustration, photographed from Gammon Head, her cargo is being discharged into a barge, which can just be seen behind her port quarter. Prawle Point coastguards under Lt Coward rowed out to the scene of the wreck in their own boat and were joined by the Salcombe lifeboat, but their services were not required as the two passengers and twenty-three crew, all Greeks apart from three British engineer officers, had landed on the rocks in their own boats. On 22 July, the *Kingsbridge Gazette* reported that all hope of getting her off the rocks had been abandoned after she had been badly damaged by heavy seas breaking right over her on 19 July.

The *Maria* was only a year old, having been launched at Sunderland in May of the preceding year. Her registered tonnage was 1,655.

SERICA

The fine lines of the wrecked steamer *Serica* show that her builders had not entirely forsaken the beauty of the sailing ship. Rigged as a fore and aft schooner, she carried on her clipper bow a figurehead which is today in the Valhalla Maritime Museum on Tresco in the Isles of Scilly. The *Serica* was run aground near the Woolpack beacon after striking an uncharted rock when leaving St Mary's on 24 November 1893, and she is seen here a total wreck with her funnel already washed overboard. She had earlier, on the 19th, put into Scilly with heavy weather damage in the course of a voyage from Cardiff to Port Said with a cargo of coal.

The *Serica* was built at Sunderland in 1888 and had a registered tonnage of 1,736.

A.C.L.

The picturesque French brig *A.C.L.*, registered at Nantes, ran ashore in dense fog on Woolacombe Sands on 25 January 1894 while bound from Bordeaux to Cardiff in ballast. Her crew of six were brought safely ashore by the breeches buoy of the Woolacombe Life Saving Apparatus Brigade. Fortunately, the *A.C.L.* was refloated several days later and towed round to Ilfracombe. She is pictured beached in the harbour with her broken mainmast bearing testimony to her recent ordeal. Her painted ports are a reminder of the days when merchant ships carried cannon for their own defence.

Built at Nantes by J. Sevestre in 1875, she had a gross tonnage of 242, a length of 96 ft, a beam of 24 ft and a depth of 12 ft. Her owners were the Cie Nationale d'Armement.

Five seamen can be seen still clinging to the rigging of the Glasgow-registered steamer *Escurial,* while the crew of the Hayle lifeboat stand helpless on Portreath beach, unable to launch their boat into the surf driven in by the NNW gale. The date is 25 January 1895 and the *Escurial,* bound from Cardiff for Fiume with a cargo of coal, had been driven ashore after a leak had put out her stokehold fires. Efforts to get a line aboard by rockets had failed and watchers on shore saw the crew being swept one by one into the sea, until finally both masts collapsed. Coastguards and lifeboat men, assisted by scores of onlookers, repeatedly dashed into the breakers and managed to pull seven of the *Escurial's* crew of eighteen to safety.

Built at Govan in 1879 for W. H. Raeburn of Glasgow, the *Escurial's* gross tonnage was 1,185 and her main dimensions were: length 230 ft, breadth 30 ft, depth 22 ft. Schooner-rigged, she carried sails to supplement her 130 hp engine.

SAINTONGE

Shortly after 3 am on 21 March 1895 a labourer living in a clifftop cottage above St Loy Bay, between Lamorna Cove and Porthcurno, heard the crash as the French steamer *Saintonge*, of La Rochelle, hit the rocks below in a dense fog. He alerted the coastguards at Penberth and the crew of the stranded ship were brought safely ashore. The *Saintonge,* which had been bound from La Rochelle to Barry Dock with a cargo of pitprops, became a total wreck after an unsuccessful attempt to tow her off on 31 March by the salvage vessels *Chase* and *Belos.* The headland seen in the picture is Boscawen Point.

The *Saintonge* was 1,642 tons gross with a length of 259 ft, a breadth of 38 ft and depth of 17 ft. She was built at Sunderland in 1882 by J. Bulmer & Co and owned by Delmas Frères of La Rochelle.

ARABELLA

Fluky winds, caused by the close proximity of the tall cliffs surrounding the harbour, frequently led to small sailing craft stranding near the entrance to Ilfracombe while attempting to navigate the tricky passage in or out of that port. One such casualty is shown here, perched high and dry on Britton Rock at the southern side of the entrance to the harbour. She is the ketch *Arabella*, of Gloucester, which grounded and became a total wreck on 2 October 1895. Her crew of four and two local men who were aboard at the time were drowned. Of 70 tons register, the *Arabella* was built far up the River Severn at the little village of Saul in 1864.

At 6 pm on 20 September 1896 a large ship was seen to be in distress off Portreath and drifting westwards with most of her sails blown away. Both St Ives and Hayle lifeboats were launched but neither was able to make contact with the casualty, the Hayle boat being driven back by the huge seas breaking on the bar. In the gathering darkness the St Ives LSA followed her along the clifftops until just before midnight, when she stranded on the eastern side of Gurnard's Head. The rescuers managed to get their second rocket into her rigging and all nineteen of her crew came off by breeches buoy. The ship was the *Alexander Yeats*, of Liverpool, carrying a cargo of timber from Sable, Savannah, to Devonport.

Built at Portland, New Brunswick, in 1876 by D. Lynch, the *Alexander Yeats'* registered tonnage was 1,589. She was owned by G. Windron of Liverpool, and her principal dimensions were: length 218·2 ft, breadth 20·2 ft, depth 24 ft.

THYRA

The Danish barquentine *Thyra* is pictured here a total wreck on the rocks at Cleave Strand, about four miles south-west of Bude. An interesting feature on her deck, behind her broken foremast, is the small windmill used for pumping. The *Thyra*, registered at Ronne and carrying a cargo of coal and bricks from Llanelly for Stockholm, went ashore on 26 October 1896 after her sails had been torn to shreds in a westerly gale. Bude lifeboat rowed out to her and took off her crew of nine, landing them at Boscastle as the seas were too rough to return to Bude. Later in the day, when the storm abated, the lifeboat took five of the crew back to their ship in the hope of saving her, but she again had to be abandoned shortly before hitting the rocks.

GILES LANG

A graphic photograph of rescue operations in progress on the sands at Maer Lake, near Bude, on 8 November 1896 when the schooner *Giles Lang* had been run aground in a NNW gale after springing a serious leak. The LSA brigade have set up their tripod, but the whip and hawser lying snake-like on the sands indicates that there had been trouble with the apparatus. To the right of the schooner rescuers are wading into the breakers, and through their efforts the crew were brought safely ashore.

The *Giles Lang,* owned and captained by Daniel Hollow of St Ives, had been bound from Porthcawl to Penzance with 200 tons of coal. She went completely to pieces on the evening tide of the same day. Built at Padstow in 1864, and of 124 tons register, she was one of twenty-nine vessels built by Tredwen between the years 1858-70.

In this panoramic view photographed in 1899 from Lower Sharpnose Point, the long westerly swell from the Atlantic is sweeping past a wrecked ship into Stanbury Mouth. The headland in the background is Higher Sharpnose Point, which lies about two miles ssw of the boundary between Cornwall and Devon. The ship is the Italian steamer *Voorwarts*, of Genoa, which drifted there on 4 January 1899 after being abandoned in a wsw gale off Trevose Head. The captain and ten of his crew left her in two boats and were never heard of again, but the remaining nine crew members were taken off by the Newquay lifeboat.

The *Voorwarts*, which later became a total wreck, was built in 1874 by John Elder & Co at Glasgow for the Netherlands Steamship Co, and sold in 1898 to G. B. Lavarello, of Genoa, without change of name. Her gross tonnage was 2,802 and, like most steamers of that period, she was long and slim, her breadth being only 37ft, compared with an overall length of 368 ft. She was propelled by an engine of 1,600 ihp.

UMBRE

The tug *Etna* and the salvage vessel *Hermes* are carrying out salvage work on the Cork-registered steamer *Umbre*. She went ashore under Chypraze Cliff about half a mile east of Pendeen Watch at 6 am on 20 February 1899 during a thick fog. The crew of nineteen took to the two boats, seven landing safely in nearby Portheras Cove and the remainder being picked up by the Brixham trawler *Evangelist*. The *Umbre*, which had been bound from Liverpool to Amsterdam with a general cargo, became a total wreck. The dangerous Three Stone Oar Rocks, known locally as The Wra, can be seen in the background of the photo.

Owned by the Cork Steamship Co Ltd, the *Umbre* was built at Newcastle in 1898 by Wigham Richardson & Co. Her main dimensions were 255×34×19 ft, and her gross tonnage was 1,312.

LLANDAFF

The small steam-coaster *Llandaff*, of Cardiff, went ashore in Nanjizal Bay, near the Land's End, during the night of 27 April 1899, after losing her bearings in the thick fog prevailing at the time. The crew of the *Llandaff*, which was bound from Sheerness to her home port in ballast, landed safely in their own boats. She is seen here with her bow hard against Diamond Horse Rock lying inside the headland of Carn Boel. This relatively sheltered position saved her, and she joined the small, select band of ships to be refloated from the Land's End area when, on 9 May, she was pulled off and towed to Penzance for repairs by the West of England Salvage Association's *Greencastle*.

The *Llandaff* was built of iron at Wallsend back in 1865, her age being reflected by her open bridge structure and turtleback bow. Her gross tonnage was 420 and she was 152 ft long, with a beam of 24 ft. She was owned by J. T. Short of Cardiff and her attractive funnel marking featured the Cornish coat-of-arms. (See also p. 33).

On 21 May 1899 the United States liner *Paris*, of New York, ran aground in misty weather at Lowland Point, near Coverack. Bound from Cherbourg for New York with general cargo, a crew of 370 and 386 passengers, she was the largest vessel to have stranded on the English coast up to that time. All the passengers were taken off by the Porthoustock and Falmouth lifeboats and then transferred to tugs and landed at Falmouth. After a tricky salvage operation, the *Paris* was pulled off the rocks by a fleet of tugs on 13 July and towed to Falmouth for temporary repairs. In November of the same year she was towed to Harland & Wolff's Belfast yard where she was almost completely rebuilt and renamed *Philadelphia*. In 1917 she became the United States armed transport *Harrisburg* and then, in 1925, she was sold to the New York–Naples Steamship Co for use as an emigrant ship. She was scrapped in Italy shortly afterwards.

With a gross tonnage of 10,449, a length of 560 ft and a beam of 63·2 ft, she had been built by J. & G. Thomson at Clydebank in 1888 as the *City of Paris* for the old Inman Line. In 1889 she gained the Blue Riband of the Atlantic, making the crossing from Queenstown to Sandy Hook in 5 days 23 hours 7 minutes.

LLANDAFF

The old *Llandaff,* having survived the stranding on the Cornish coast earlier in the year, was driven ashore near the Barrel Rock at Bude on 2 October 1899 during a NW gale. The crew of eleven were brought ashore by the Bude Rocket Apparatus Brigade. The *Llandaff,* which had been bound from St Malo to Swansea, was driven further inshore on the next tide, which left her in the precarious position shown in the photograph with her bow high in the air over the old swimming pool. The coaster, which at that time was under the new ownership of Morgan Wakley & Co, was later refloated, but this time she was towed to Cardiff for scrapping.

2 TWENTIETH-CENTURY SHIPWRECKS

Only a few hours after this photograph was taken, the ketch *Star,* of Scilly, had completely disappeared, broken up by a heavy NNW gale. Bound from Cardiff to the Scilly Isles with a cargo of coal, she ran for St Ives Harbour for shelter on 6 November 1900, but failed to get inside and dragged her anchors onto Pedn-Olva Rocks. The St Ives lifeboat was launched at 7.30 am and took off her crew of three. Her loss was a tragedy for her owners, Banfield & Hooper of Scilly, as neither the vessel nor her cargo were insured.

The *Star* was built at St Mary's in the Scilly Isles by John Edwards in 1857 as a two-masted dandy with a registered tonnage of 48. She was lengthened in 1867, her registered tonnage being increased to 68 and her dimensions to 73·4 × 17·2 × 8·6 ft.

MARIE CELINE

On the western side of Nare Head, in Gerrans Bay, lies a small inlet known locally as Parada Cove. This for a while became the resting place of the French schooner *Marie Celine,* of Nantes, which went ashore there on 19 January 1901 after being blown back from a position off the Manacles in a sw gale. As the ship grounded, one of the crew jumped overboard with a rope and the rest were able to save themselves with its aid.

The schooner, built at Nantes in 1892, was on a voyage from Southampton to Gijon with a cargo of pitch. Although badly damaged, she was eventually refloated, repaired and registered at Truro as owned by William Bryant. She traded into the 1930s, surviving three strandings altogether.

JULIEN MARIE

To be caught in a gale on a lee shore was the fear of every sailing-ship master, especially when there was no natural safe haven to make for, as was the case on the North Cornish coast. In a report presented to both Houses of Parliament in 1906, in which it was recommended that a harbour of refuge should be built at St Ives, no less than 399 ships were listed as having foundered or stranded in the area from Land's End to Hartland Point from 1 July 1884 to 6 March 1903.

Among these casualties was the French brigantine *Julien Marie,* of Auray, seen here on Porthminster beach at St Ives where she became a total wreck. Bound from Swansea to France with a cargo of 162 tons of coal, she was caught in a heavy NNE gale on 5 February 1901 and tried unsuccessfully to run for the safety of St Ives harbour. The local lifeboat took off her crew of six, together with their pet dog, just before she ran ashore. In the photograph, the mainmast of the brigantine can be seen lying in the surf near Pedn-Olva Point. Immediately above it, on the rocks, the curiously shaped building is an old mine engine house built in 1860 although no shaft was ever sunk there.

Crowds of interested spectators from Perranporth have come down onto Perran Beach to inspect the latest wreck, driven ashore near Droskyn Point in a NW gale on 7 March 1901. The ship was the Dutch barquentine *Voorspoed*, of Amsterdam, bound from Cardiff to Bahia in South America with coal and general cargo. Her crew were brought ashore by breeches buoy after a rocket line had been fired over the wreck right into the teeth of the gale. In the photograph the *Voorspoed* is temporarily out of reach of the breakers which drove her on to the beach. On her deck can be seen the helmeted figures of three policemen, there no doubt because of the looting which had been reported by her captain. The *Voorspoed*, built of steel at Martenshoek in 1892 as the *Jan Derks*, was refloated two weeks later by the well-known Falmouth tug *Triton*, but on her next voyage she disappeared with all hands while bound for Newfoundland.

The camera has caught the sea in a peaceful mood at the Lizard on a fine summer's day in 1902, but the wrecked steamer *St Aubyn*, lying in Housel Bay, is a reminder that this most southerly point in England has taken a dreadful toll of shipping over the centuries. The *St Aubyn*, bound from Cardiff to London with coal, struck the Stags on 20 August and was beached in Housel Bay to prevent her from sinking. The photograph shows her cargo being discharged into sailing barges, overlooked by the old Lizard Signal Station on Pen Olver Point. The *St Aubyn*, which was later towed to Falmouth for repairs, was registered at London and owned by E. C. Nichols. She was built at Wallsend in 1875 with a length of 235 ft, a beam of 32 ft and a gross tonnage of 1,195.

VESPER

The crew of the Brixham fishing smack *Vesper* are here seen salvaging as much removable gear as possible from their stranded vessel before the sea completes its destruction. The smack ran onto the rocks half a mile north-west of Black Head, near Ansteys Cove, Torquay, in a dense fog at 5·30 am on Friday, 12 December 1902. Her crew were able to row ashore in their own lifeboat, but the ship herself, which was insured for £280, became a total loss.

The *Vesper,* owned by Captain J. H. Bovey of Brixham, had a length of 56·5 ft, a breadth of 15·4 ft, a depth of 7·7 ft, and a registered tonnage of 24. She was built in 1892 by Robert Jackman in the Victoria Shipbuilding Yard which was situated behind Brixham breakwater. All signs of the yard have long since disappeared, and today the area is known as Breakwater Beach, sun-worshippers having replaced the craftsmen of the shipyard.

BENWICK

Situated off the south-westerly tip of the Land's End Peninsula is the Runnelstone. Among the many ships which have come to grief on this reef was the steamer *Benwick,* of Liverpool. Bound from Antwerp to Swansea in ballast, she hit the rocks on 11 February 1903 during a thick fog. Twenty-four of her crew took to the boats, but the captain, the two mates, the chief engineer and one fireman remained on board. The steamer got off the rocks but as she began to settle by the bow, Sennen Cove lifeboat took off these five men. However, the *Benwick* stayed afloat long enough to drift ashore near Porthcurno, where she is pictured above, a total wreck.

Built at Wallsend in 1889, the *Benwick* was owned by J. W. Thompson. She had a gross tonnage of 2,773, a length of 302 ft, a breadth of 40 ft and a depth of 20 ft.

CRYSTAL SPRING
(facing page, above)

The battered timbers of the once beautiful two-masted schooner *Crystal Spring* are here seen set against the striking background of the contorted rock strata of Maer Cliff, north of Bude. The schooner went aground on 25 August 1904 in a northerly gale after missing stays while coming into Bude from Garston with a cargo of coal. The crew were hauled to safety in the breeches buoy, watched by a large crowd that had raced to the scene with the Bude Life Saving Apparatus Brigade.

Registered at Preston, the *Crystal Spring* was built at Tarleton in 1870 with a registered tonnage of 60 and was owned by John Hoey of Annagassan, County Louth, Ireland.

KING CADWALLON

Islanders from St Martins in the Scilly Isles have rowed out to investigate the
steamer *King Cadwallon*, wrecked on the Hard Lewis Rocks, half a mile off
St Martins Head. Some have boarded the wreck and are attempting to salvage
one of the ship's boats by lowering it over the port side. The *King Cadwallon*,
bound from Barry to Naples with 5,000 tons of coal, ran onto the rocks at 5 am on
22 July 1906 after dense fog had prevailed almost continually since she had sailed.
The crew of twenty-seven escaped in one of the ship's boats.

Built at Port Glasgow in 1900 and with a registered tonnage of 2,126, the *King
Cadwallon* later slipped off the rocks and sank. Her port of registry was London
and she was owned by the King Line.

JEBBA

All 155 passengers and crew were hauled to safety by breeches buoy across the stretch of water seen in this photograph between the steeply sloping cliffs and the wrecked Elder Dempster liner *Jebba*. The liner, homeward bound from Sierra Leone, went ashore at Whitechurch, near Bolt Tail, in dense fog in the early hours of 18 March 1907. In those days there was a lifeboat stationed at nearby Hope Cove, but she was unable to help as seas were breaking over the decks of the liner and rocks blocked the passage to the sheltered port side. In the darkness two local men, Isaac Jarvis and John Argeat, climbed down the 200ft cliffs and rigged a bosun's chair to effect the rescue. Both were later awarded the Albert Medal by King Edward VII.

The *Jebba*, which had been built as the *Albertville* in 1896 by Sir R. Dixion & Co at Middlesbrough, became a total wreck, although the mails and much of her rubber and ivory cargo were salvaged. Of 3,813 tons gross, she was 352 ft in length with a beam of 44·2 ft. In 1971 a skin diver found one of her dining-room plates, patterned on which was her original name of *Albertville*.

42

TEHWIJA

Locals from Exmouth are walking along the beach to Orecombe Point to view the shattered remains of the three-masted Russian schooner *Tehwija*, of Riga, wrecked on 10 October 1907. She had been waiting outside Exmouth for a pilot with a cargo of 302 tons of timber destined for that port from Lappvik, in Finland, but had been blown ashore by a SSE gale which had suddenly sprung up. Exmouth lifeboat found it impossible to row against the wind and seas but, luckily, the Teignmouth lifeboat was able to reach the scene and in a remarkable rescue pulled all eight members of the *Tehwija*'s crew through the sea to the lifeboat by throwing lines to them. The cargo, which was strewn all along the beach, was collected and later sold by auction at Exmouth Docks.

The *Tehwija* had been built at Kaleten in 1890 by Kirstein, and at the time of her loss was owned by A. O. Damen of Svarta. Her length was 122 ft and her registered tonnage was 204.

HUDDERSFIELD

The battered remains of the tramp steamer *Huddersfield*, of Cardiff, lie under the cliffs about one mile east of Hartland Point, where she was wrecked on 27 January 1908. Bound from Barry to the River Plate with 3,000 tons of coal, she went ashore at 4.15 am in thick fog. Nine of her crew took to one of their boats and rowed to Clovelly to raise the alarm. Clovelly lifeboat was launched and in a timely and spectacular rescue took off the remaining twelve crew members despite the huge seas that were sweeping over the decks of the wreck.

The *Huddersfield*, of 2,055 tons gross, was built at Sunderland in 1900 and was 289 ft in length, with a beam of 43 ft.

HODBARROW MINOR
(above left)

A tragic shipwreck occurred at Mawgan Porth, near Newquay, on 6 March 1908, when the topsail schooner *Hodbarrow Minor* was deliberately run aground in an attempt to save lives. After her captain had been washed overboard off the Longships, an able seaman named Joseph Warricker, of Falmouth, took command and decided to beach the schooner after running before a force 10 gale from the northwest. He and the other three remaining crew members launched the ship's boat as the schooner struck, but this overturned and only Warricker managed to struggle through the surf to safety.

The *Hodbarrow Minor*, which had been bound from Runcorn to Truro with coal, was built at Ulverston in 1871. Of 99 tons register, she had a length of 89 ft and a beam of 21 ft. At the time of her loss she was owned by James Fisher.

GIRL ANNIE
(above right)

The crew of the Lowestoft sailing smack *Girl Annie* can here be seen trying to save their belongings and fishing gear from their tiny vessel, trapped on huge boulders in a cove under Trevilley Cliff, about a mile SE of Land's End. Within a few hours of this photograph being taken, the smack had been smashed to pieces by the incoming tide. Earlier, at 3 am on 4 May 1908, the *Girl Annie* had gone aground in dense fog and her crew had got away in the ship's boat, to land safely in Nanjizal Bay.

The *Girl Annie* had been built in 1902 for J. Bond, of Lowestoft, by Gibbs & Co at their picturesque shipyard in Galmpton Creek on the River Dart. Her gross tonnage was 61, length 72·0 ft, beam 18·7 ft and depth 8·9 ft.

CROSSOWEN

The Glasgow-registered brigantine *Crossowen* lies awash on Yarmer Sands, near Thurlestone, South Devon, her masts and yards appearing to dwarf the distant cliffs of Bolt Tail. She ran ashore in dense fog during the early hours of 7 May 1908 when bound from Par to Leith with a cargo of china clay. Tragically, her crew of seven were found drowned at the mouth of the River Avon, the ship's boat apparently having overturned in the surf on Bantham Bar.

The *Crossowen*, which became a total wreck, was built at Grangemouth in 1878 by Adamson as the *Omega*. She was 115 ft in length and had a gross tonnage of 237. At the time of her loss she was owned by W. C. Phillips of St Austell, Cornwall.

MADELEINE

The camera has recorded the fashions of 1908 in this photograph of a small group of people standing by the stranded French schooner *Madeleine*, of Fecamp. She was run ashore on the sands under the famous Pebble Ridge of Westward Ho on the night of 31 August of that year, after she had lost nearly all her sails in a gale in Bideford Bay while bound from Swansea to her home port with a cargo of coal. Her crew of five landed over her bows as the tide ebbed and spent the remainder of the night on Northam Burrows as no-one had seen the schooner come ashore. The *Madeleine*, built at Fecamp and of 149 tons gross, was later refloated and repaired at Appledore, North Devon.

46

INFATIGABLE

The Russian wooden barque *Infatigable* is seen here ashore under St Mawes Castle, near Falmouth, after she had dragged her anchors during a SW gale on the night of 23 January 1910. Bound from London to Cardiff in ballast, and in tow of the tug *Challenge*, she had failed to get around the Land's End because of the bad weather and had put back to Falmouth for shelter. On the next high tide, the *Challenge*, reinforced by the local tugs *Dragon*, *Marian* and *Briton*, refloated the barque but she was so badly damaged that she was abandoned by her owners. Later, she was towed to London and on arriving there on 30 March she was sold by auction for £800, to be broken up.

The *Infatigable* was built in 1884 by A. Knudsen at Grimstad for M. Falck, of Arendal. Her gross tonnage was 871, and her main dimensions were: length 180·5 ft, breadth 34·8 ft, depth of hold 20 ft. She had several changes of ownership during her life, until in 1910 she was finally sold to A/S Infatigable and managed by M. Kramer of Abo, Russia (now Turku, in Finland).

HARRY

With her sails still set, the Brixham ketch-rigged sailing trawler *Harry* lies hard against the granite rocks of Rospletha Cliff, near Porthcurno, in Cornwall. She went ashore at 2.45 am on 13 March 1910 during a southerly gale. Coastguards saw her distress flares and called out Sennen Cove lifeboat, which eventually picked up her crew of four from the small boat in which they had left the wreck. The *Harry*, which had been built at Brixham in 1904 by S. J. Dewdney, became a total wreck. Her length was 66·8 ft, beam 18·5 ft and depth 8·8 ft.

WILLIAM CORY

A photographer climbed down the cliff near Levant mine, about one mile south-west of Pendeen lighthouse, in Cornwall, to take this spectacular view of the steamer *William Cory*. The ebbing tide has left her perched on rocks with her rudder and propeller high out of the water, whilst on her deck are stacked thousands of pit props which she was carrying from Uleaborg to Newport for use in the Welsh coalmines. The *William Cory* had been deliberately run aground as she was leaking badly after striking the Vynecs, off Cape Cornwall, in clear fine weather on 5 September 1910. Her crew rowed ashore in the ship's boats, but the steamer became a total wreck.

The *William Cory* had been built only the previous year by S. P. Austin at Sunderland. Of 2,660 tons gross, her length was 314 ft, breadth 45·2 ft and depth 20·7 ft. She was owned by the well-known collier firm of the same name.

OLYMPE

When the thirty three-year-old French schooner *Olympe*, of Lannion, came ashore at Gunwalloe Church Cove, in Cornwall, shortly after 5 am on Sunday, 3 October 1910, workers and holiday-makers staying at nearby Poldhu Hotel rushed down to the cove and helped the crew of five ashore by forming a human chain in the surf breaking on the beach. The *Olympe* had been blown ashore in a sw gale while bound from her home port to Swansea, with pitprops. In the picture, taken from Poldhu Point, the storm-battered schooner is seen against the background of the weatherbeaten 600-year-old church with its isolated tower, protected from the sea by the wall built into the sand.

ANGELE

With her sails in tatters and with most of the planking torn away from her bulwarks, the French brigantine *Angele* lies abandoned on the dreaded Doom Bar at the entrance to Padstow Harbour. She went ashore after running back up Channel for shelter from a strong WNW gale on 12 October 1911, while bound from Swansea to L'Orient with a cargo of coal and bricks. Four of her crew were swept overboard and drowned, only her captain being saved by the Padstow lifeboat which, earlier in the day, had saved the crew of five from the schooner *Island Maid*, also wrecked on the Doom Bar.

SALUTO
(facing page, below)

A sw swell running into Mounts Bay crashes against the side of the Norwegian iron barque *Saluto,* ashore in a severe gale on 13 December 1911. Bound from London to Barbados in ballast, she was driven into Perran Boat Cove by mountainous seas even though she had dropped both anchors after her sails had been blown into shreds. In an exciting rescue, the Newlyn lifeboat *Elizabeth and Blanche* took off her crew of thirteen shortly before the barque grounded.

The *Saluto*, registered at Christiansand and owned by S. O. Stray, became a total wreck. She was built back in 1867 by T. Dubigeon at Nantes as the *National,* later being renamed *Minna Cords* and, finally, *Saluto.*

CITY OF CARDIFF

A member of the crew swings perilously in the breeches buoy as huge seas, swept by a wnw gale, batter the steamer *City of Cardiff,* in Nanjizal Bay, near the Land's End, on 21 March 1912. All the crew of twenty-two, the wife of the captain and the two-year-old-son and wife of the chief officer were hauled to safety by the Sennen Rocket Brigade. The *City of Cardiff,* bound from Le Havre to Cardiff in ballast, soon became a total wreck and her boilers, covered by seaweed, can still be seen at low water.

The steamer was built at Stockton in 1906 by Ropner & Co, and her gross tonnage was 3,089. Owned by the Instow Steamship Co Ltd, she had a length of 330·5 ft, a breadth of 48 ft and a depth of 21·7 ft.

GUNVOR

Having made the long journey from Caleta Buena, in Chile, with her cargo of nitrates, the Norwegian three-masted steel barque *Gunvor,* of Fredrickstadt, has become a victim of fog only a few miles from her destination, the port of Falmouth. With most of her sails set, she blundered into Beagles Hole, near Black Head, south-west of Coverack, on 6 April 1912. The seas were calm and her crew were able to lower a ladder over the bows and scramble onto the rocks, but the barque, originally built as the *General Mellinet,* became a total wreck.

INDUSTRY

On Friday, 27 September 1912, the barquentine *Industry*, of Swansea, was sighted off Padstow, North Cornwall, flying distress signals after springing a serious leak while bound from Britonferry to Treport. To save her from sinking, Captain Everett ran her aground in Harlyn Bay. The crew of six were able to row ashore in their own boat. The cargo of 320 tons of coal was offloaded into horse-drawn carts and sold to local merchants, but the *Industry* was sold for scrap and dismantled on the beach.

She was an old ship, having been built as long ago as 1857 at St John, New Brunswick. Her gross tonnage was 212 and her length 108 ft, with a beam of 24 ft. At the time of her loss she was owned by G. Shepherd, of Swansea. In the photograph Gunver Head and Stepper Point can be seen to the right of the *Industry*, with Gulland Rock lying on the horizon to the left.

Considered by many experts to be one of the fastest and most beautiful sailing ships of her day, the four-masted steel barque *Queen Margaret* is pictured here going to her grave on the Stags reef, off the Lizard Point. One hundred and thirty days out from Sydney with a cargo of wheat, she arrived at the Lizard on 5 May 1913 only to run onto the rocks in perfectly calm weather through her captain standing in too close for the purpose of speaking to the lighthouse. To quote Basil Lubbock, 'There can seldom have been a more stupid and unnecessary end to a ship than that of the beautiful *Queen Margaret*.' Fortunately, her crew of twenty-six, the captain's wife and her baby, all came ashore safely in nearby Polpeor Cove, some in the ship's boat and the remainder in the Lizard lifeboat.

Built by Macmillan at Dumbarton in 1893, the *Queen Margaret* had a gross tonnage of 2,144 and was owned by J. A. Black, of Glasgow.

CROMDALE

Huge seas whipped up by a ssw gale are completing the destruction of the magnificent full-rigged ship *Cromdale*, of Aberdeen, which had run aground at the Lizard a week earlier, on 23 May 1913. She went ashore during dense fog on Bass Point, almost immediately under Lloyds signal station, when very nearly at the end of her voyage from Taltal, Chile, to Falmouth for orders with a cargo of nitrates. Distress rockets soon brought the Cadgwith and Lizard lifeboats to the scene, and the crew of twenty-four and the captain's wife were brought safely ashore.

The *Cromdale* was built by Barclay Curle & Co at Glasgow in 1891. Owned by W. Westland Rose, she had a registered tonnage of 1,849.

KATINA

The Greek steamer *Katina* went ashore on a high spring tide under Elmscott Cliffs, a mile and a half south of Hartland Quay, during a dense fog on the night of 23 May 1913. She was bound from Athens to Barry Docks in ballast. Her plight was not discovered until daylight the next morning, but by then her crew had walked ashore as the tide receded and scaled the 400 ft high cliffs. The *Katina* was one of the few lucky ships to survive being stranded on this treacherous stretch of coast. She was towed off by the tug *Etna* on 5 May and beached at Clovelly. Here, temporary repairs were carried out to her damaged hull by the Cornish firm of Chennells before she was towed to Cardiff.

Owned by J. Goumas, the *Katina* was built as the *Dowgate* at the Swan Hunter yard at Wallsend in 1895. Constructed of steel, she had a gross tonnage of 2,899, a length of 327 ft and a beam of 41 ft.

ALMA

The ebbing tide has enabled the crew of the 91-ton German schooner *Alma*, of Bremen, to return to their stranded ship to secure the sails and rigging. The schooner was driven ashore in a sw gale on Crinnis Beach in St Austell Bay on 13 May 1913, after breaking adrift from her tug while on passage to Par from Newhaven with a cargo of cement. Captain Westerholt and his crew of five were taken off by breeches buoy just before the Polkerris lifeboat reached the scene. Luckily, the *Alma* was undamaged and was later pulled off the beach by the Falmouth tug *Perran*, under Captain W. White.

VOLONTAIRE

The French schooner *Volontaire* lies high and dry on the foreshore of the little fishing village of Polkerris, on the eastern side of St Austell Bay. She was blown ashore on 30 May 1913 after her cables had parted in heavy seas and a strong sw gale. A lifeboat was stationed at Polkerris from 1862 until 1922, and the lifeboatmen helped the crew of the schooner ashore with the aid of ropes thrown to the stranded vessel. The old lifeboat house can be seen just to the right of the bowsprit of the *Volontaire*.

VILLE DU TEMPLE

Half a mile off the coastal road from St Ives to the Land's End, between Gurnard's Head and Morvah, lies the splendid headland of Bosigran Castle. Its western edge drops precipitously into Porthmoina Cove, where the French steamer *Ville du Temple* was found wrecked in 1913. She had been abandoned by her crew after she had struck the Runnelstone in dense fog on 29 November 1913, but had stayed afloat to drift all the way around the Land's End peninsula. She was on a voyage from Nantes to Cardiff in ballast. Her crew of twenty-three were picked up by the Penzance steamer *Mercutio* and landed at St Ives.

The *Ville du Temple* was built at Sunderland in 1889 by J. L. Thompson & Sons as the *Cambria* for the International Line Steamship Co Ltd. She had a gross tonnage of 2,047 and a length of 284 ft. In 1910 she was sold to Cie des Chargeurs Français, of Bayonne, and renamed *Ville du Temple*.

ASNIERES

The beautiful four-masted French barque *Asnieres,* of Le Havre, went aground at St Mawes at noon on 2 December 1914, in a SE gale. She was entering Falmouth for orders after a voyage from San Francisco with a cargo of barley. At first her crew remained aboard, but two days later, when the weather deteriorated, twenty-five were taken off by the Falmouth lifeboat.

The *Asnieres* of 3,103 tons gross and built at her home port in 1902, was refloated early in the new year by the West of England Salvage Co. She was finally lost some two years later when, on 2 January 1917, she was sunk by the German armed raider *Moewe* near St Paul's Rocks.

ENSIGN

Fishermen and port officials have rowed out from Salcombe, in Devon, to inspect the wreck of the wooden schooner *Ensign,* of Plymouth, lying on the Blackstone Rock at the entrance to the estuary. Only her masts are now showing above the water. Carrying a cargo of coal and iron from Glasgow to Salcombe, she hit the rocks and foundered on 30 January 1915. Her crew of four were saved.

Built at Barmouth in 1883, the *Ensign* had a gross tonnage of 116. She was 87.0 ft in length, with a beam of 21.3 ft and a depth of 10.2 ft.

ANDROMEDA
(*facing page, above*)

After running the gauntlet of enemy submarines with her badly needed cargo of 2,500 tons of grain, taken aboard at Tacoma, in Oregon, the London-registered barque *Andromeda* was totally wrecked in a sw gale on Killygerran Head, near Portscatho, Cornwall on 12 February 1915. An apprentice was washed overboard and drowned, but the remainder of the crew, including the captain's wife, his ten-year-old daughter, and his wife's sister of eighteen, were brought safely ashore by breeches buoy manned by Territorials encamped in a nearby field.

In a letter to the author, the second mate of the *Andromeda* has described how he and 'seven others were very kindly entertained by Squire Spry at his big house and we were all wearing his summer suits while ours dried; eating two good meals— one when we arrived at 3.30 am and breakfast at 8 am. And bless my soul if he didn't give us 2s 6d each when we left for Falmouth, just to buy cigarettes with! What a kindly man!'

The *Andromeda,* of 1,762 tons register, was built by Duncans of Port Glasgow in 1890.

FLORA
(*facing page, below*)

The Dutch steamer *Flora,* with her name and port of registry painted in large letters on her sides to denote her neutrality, was a World War I wreck on the North Devon coast on 4 April 1915, while on passage from Amsterdam to Swansea in ballast. She drove ashore in fog close under the 200 ft high cliffs of Longpeak, about two miles south of Hartland Point. Wisely, the crew of nineteen decided not to launch the ship's boats into the heavy swell that was breaking on the rocks around their stranded ship, and were later able to walk safely ashore as the tide ebbed.

Owned by the Royal Netherlands Steamship Co, the *Flora* was built at Rotterdam in 1894. She had a gross tonnage of 725, a length of 200 ft, a beam of 28 ft and was equipped with a 96 hp engine.

NEWTOWN

Another World War I wreck, the steamer *Newtown*, of London, is seen here perched amidships on a rock between Barracane Beach and Harris's Cove, near Woolacombe, North Devon. She went ashore on 7 January 1916 while bound from Oporto to Newport with a cargo of pitprops. Her crew were rescued by breeches buoy but the steamer herself became a total wreck, and was broken up for scrap by a local firm of contractors. Most of her cargo was washed ashore on neighbouring beaches and salvaged.

Built by J. Crown & Sons Ltd at Sunderland in the year preceding her wreck, the *Newtown* was owned by Town Line (London) Ltd. Her gross tonnage was 1,153.

YVONNE

Plymouth breakwater, completed in 1848 and built to protect the shipping in Plymouth Sound from the prevailing sw gales, has itself been the site of a number of shipwrecks. One of these was the French four-masted barquentine *Yvonne,* of Marseilles, strikingly portrayed here with only the stumps of her fore and mizzen masts remaining. She was driven onto the breakwater in a se gale on 3 October 1920. Her crew of nineteen jumped onto the breakwater and, later, all but one were safely transferred to the Plymouth lifeboat and the tug *Rover.*

The *Yvonne* was built of wood by H. D. Bendixen of Eureka, California, in 1900 as the *John Palmer* and her gross tonnage was 1,120.

MARGUERITE

The French steam trawler *Marguerite,* of Boulogne, was on her way to Plymouth with her holds full of fish when she ran aground in Talland Bay, west of Looe, Cornwall, in a sw gale with poor visibility at 5.30 am on 3 March 1922. The Looe pulling lifeboat was towed to the scene of the wreck by the motor lugger *Dorothy* and took off all twenty-one of the trawler's crew. Among these was the skipper's ten-year-old son who had been strapped to his father's back since the trawler grounded to prevent him from being washed overboard. Salvage proved impossible after examination had shown that the sharp rock ledges had pounded in a number of the trawler's bottom plates.

FIMMO
(facing page)

In an attempt to lighten her for refloating, the cargo of fertilizers is being thrown overboard from the German auxiliary three-masted schooner *Fimmo,* of Geeste-munde, which stranded off Braunton, North Devon, on 1 May 1923. She was coming in over the bar when the chain on her steering gear parted and she became out of control. Some of the Appledore lifeboat crew went out in their boarding boat and took off her crew of nine. The *Fimmo* was later refloated and repaired at Appledore.

Built at Boitzenburg in 1917 by F. Lemm for W. Schuchmann, the *Fimmo* had a gross tonnage of 464 and was 154 ft in length. In 1934 she was sold to Pio Bonucelli of Viareggio, Italy, and renamed *Fortunato Pio,* ownership passing to Umberto Tomei of the same port in 1937. She was sunk by air attack off Benghazi on 21 July 1940.

Interested spectators are dwarfed by the steamship *River Lagan* ashore on Good-rington Beach, near Paignton, South Devon, on 8 January 1924. She was on passage from Portsmouth to Swansea in ballast when she was driven ashore in a SE gale with heavy snow showers. Torquay Life Saving Apparatus Brigade fired a line over the ship and all the crew of thirteen were safely brought ashore in the breeches buoy between 5 and 8·30 am.

The *River Lagan* was owned at the time by West Glamorgan Steamers, of Swansea, having been built by R. Duncan & Co at Port Glasgow in 1882. She had a gross tonnage of 803, a length of 207 ft and a beam of 29 ft. She was refloated and, in 1927, she was sold to Palgrave Murphy of Dublin and renamed *City of Water-ford*. She did not remain in their ownership for long because, on 3 February of the same year, she became a total wreck on the Skerry Vore Rock while bound from Stornoway to Hamburg.

SMILING THRO'

Sightseers have walked across from Padstow to Trevone Bay to view the Yarmouth
steam trawler *Smiling Thro'* which ran aground there on 20 April 1924. She struck
a reef at Pentonwarra Point while making for Padstow in a thick fog. The crew of
nine landed in their own boat, but the trawler was badly holed and became a total
wreck. She had been built as HMS *Neaptide* by the Ouse Shipbuilding Co, Hook,
in 1920.

JOFFRE

Huge seas pound the South Shields steam tug *Joffre,* stranded under West Cliff, about 1½ miles SE of Bolt Tail, in South Devon, where she went aground in thick fog on 27 May 1925. The mate swam ashore with a line, and the remaining ten members of the crew were brought to safety by breeches buoy, although the tug master later died from exhaustion. The mate was subsequently presented with an award by the Royal Humane Society for his brave action. The *Joffre* was considered at first to be a total loss but she must have been well built for, miraculously, she was refloated two months later and continued towing until 1966 when she was broken up for scrap.

Owned by Lawson-Batey, the *Joffre* was built at Ardrossan in 1916 by the Ardrossan Shipbuilding Co. Of 260 tons gross, she had a length of 115 ft and was fitted with a 149-hp engine.

Many wrecks have occurred on Prawle Point, the most southerly tip of the coast of Devon. A particularly spectacular stranding occurred there in dense fog at 9.15 am on 17 August 1926, when the Dutch steamer *Betsy Anna* went right up between The Island and the mainland while bound from Fleetwood to Rotterdam in ballast. In the photograph, Gammon Head can be seen to the right, with Bolt Head stretching away in the distance. Luckily, the weather held fine and the steamer was refloated on 3 October by the tug *Trustee* and beached in Mill Bay in the Salcombe Estuary for temporary repairs. Nine days later she was towed eastwards by the *Trustee,* bound for Cowes, but on the following day, when off Portland Bill in heavy weather, the tow rope broke and the *Betsy Anna* foundered.

She was built in 1892 by W. Dobson & Co at Newcastle as the *Ashington* for the Ashington Coal Co, and was sold in 1905 to a Dutch firm who renamed her *Betsy Anna*. Of 880 tons gross, her length was 206.7 ft, breadth 30.1 ft and depth 14.1 ft.

The photographer has travelled from the mainland by boat to take this unusual view of the Greek steamship *Maria Kyriakides,* aground on Lundy Island. She ran ashore in dense fog at the Quarries, on the eastern side of the island, on 24 March 1929. Her crew of fourteen were saved. Although seriously holed, she was successfully refloated in the following year and towed to Ilfracombe, where her cargo of coal was discharged. It was not thought worthwhile repairing the damage, so she was later towed to Newport to be broken up by Cashmores.

The *Maria Kyriakides* had been built in 1921 as the *Pilton* for the Tatem Steam Navigation Co of Cardiff, with a registered tonnage of 1,848. She had been aground once before, on 27 December 1924 near Sully Island, Glamorgan. She was ashore there for four months before being refloated and towed to Barry for repairs.

NAIAD

The schooner *Naiad* dropped anchor off Looe, in South Cornwall, to wait for a pilot on 28 March 1931. Aboard she had 110 tons of granite blocks intended for Looe harbour. Just before midnight, a sudden gale blew up and she dragged her anchor, ending up on the rocks at Hannafore Point, West Looe. Her crew of five were taken off by the Looe pilot boat after a falling boom had struck one of the crew unconscious. The rocks pierced two holes in the schooner's hull and she quickly filled with water and went to pieces.

The *Naiad* had been built of iron at Llanelly by the Neville Brothers way back in 1867. Her gross tonnage was 240. At the time of her loss she was owned by Messrs. Allen & Sons of Watchet, Captain Redd of Watchet and Captain Smith of St Austell.

LYMINGE

Shortly after the kick-off at a rugby match at St Ives on the afternoon of 19 September 1931, the boom of the lifeboat maroons was heard reverberating through the thick fog. Two of the lifeboat's crew, who were also members of the local rugby team, left the field and sped down to the harbour, as did many of the spectators. The casualty was the Cardiff-registered steamer *Lyminge*, which had run on to the Ebal rocks off the extremity of Gurnard's Head while bound from Cardiff to Oporto with a cargo of coal. The lifeboat's services were not required, though, as the crew and three passengers on the *Lyminge* were able to row ashore in the ship's boats, landing in one of the nearby coves. Later some of the crew returned to the wreck to save the ship's cat.

In the photograph, the German ocean-going tug *Seefalke* is seen hovering off the stranded ship, but the *Lyminge* is already mortally wounded. Owned by Constants (South Wales) Ltd, she had been built as the *Lady Rhondda* by Wood, Skinner & Co at Newcastle in 1918 for the Plisson Steam Navigation Co Ltd of Cardiff, being sold to Constants in 1927. Her gross tonnage was 1,039 and her dimensions were: $260.4 \times 37.7 \times 16.4$ ft. Her three-cylinder engines, built by J. Dickinson & Sons of Sunderland, developed 207 hp.

Just before midnight on 17 December 1933, the Belgian steam coaster *Charles Jose,* of Antwerp, went ashore in thick mist in the middle of Slapton Sands, South Devon, while bound from Brussels to Llanelly with a cargo of scrap iron. She grounded very close to the Royal Sands Hotel, destroyed in World War II by the Allied forces during their practice invasion in the South Hams. One of the crew and the captain's wife were brought ashore by breeches buoy, and eight other crew members landed in the ship's boat. The captain elected to stay aboard and his perseverance was rewarded when, on 2 January of the following year, the *Charles Jose* was pulled off by tugs after her cargo had been jettisoned on the beach.

The coaster was built in 1899 by the Irvine Shipbuilding & Engineering Co as the *Paris,* but was renamed *Charles Jose* in 1933 when she was sold to Jan Van der Perre, of Antwerp. She was a very unlucky ship for him, capsizing and sinking four miles west of the Haaks Light Vessel on 4 October 1934. She had a gross tonnage of 551, a length of 180 ft, and a beam of 27 ft 6 in.

CICELIA

In the mid-1930s coal was still being brought to St Ives by sea. One of the last sailing ships to unload this cargo at the port was the Bideford-registered ketch *Cicelia*. She arrived from Lydney early in 1935, but on 18 January she broke her moorings on Smeaton's Pier in a NW gale and drifted onto nearby Pedn Olva Point, where she completely broke up.

The *Cicelia* had been built sixty-eight years earlier by Daniel Le Seurer, of Jersey, and for many years this little ship had sailed across the Atlantic in the Newfoundland salt cod trade, although only of 79 tons register. At the time of her loss she was owned by her master, Frederick Bennett, of Ilfracombe.

CLAN MALCOLM

The autumnal gales have swept away the funnel and most of the deck fittings from the steamer *Clan Malcolm,* of Glasgow, impaled on the Tregwin Rocks, near Cadgwith, on the Lizard Peninsula. Bound from Port Natal to the Clyde, via London, she ran aground in dense fog on the evening of 26 September 1935. The Lizard lifeboat and the German tug *Seefalke* were soon on the scene, but with 12 ft of water in her stokehold she was already doomed. The crew landed safely at Cadgwith in the ship's boats.

Built by Craig Taylor & Co at Stockton in 1917, and owned by Clan Lines, Steamers Ltd, the *Clan Malcolm* had a gross tonnage of 5,994 and engines of 560 hp.

HERZOGIN CECILIE

A poignant reminder of the graceful age of the square-rigged ship is this photograph
of the magnificent four-masted Finnish steel barque *Herzogin Cecilie*. One of the
fast diminishing fleet of sailing ships still trading, her life came to a sad end when
she grounded in Soar Mill Cove, near Salcombe, after striking the Ham Stone
early in the morning of 25 April 1936 in thick fog. Bound from Port Lincoln to
Ipswich with 4,500 tons of Australian wheat, she was under the command of
Captain Sven Eriksson. The Salcombe lifeboat took off twenty-one of her crew and
a lady passenger, and the local LSA team fired a line over the ship in the afternoon
to maintain communication with the remaining eight crew members who had
remained on board. Refloated two months later, the barque was beached in the

shelter of Starehole Cove, just outside Salcombe, so that her rotting cargo could be discharged. Unfortunately, on 17 July unseasonably bad weather resulted in a tremendous swell from the south-east being swept into the cove causing the *Herzogin Cecilie* to break her back. There she remained until 19 January 1939, when in a severe gale her four masts went by the board and she began to break up.

The *Herzogin Cecilie*, built at Bremerhaven in 1902 as a school ship for the North German Lloyd Line, had a gross tonnage of 3,242 and was 314 ft in length. After being sold to Gustaf Erickson of Mariehamm in 1921, she won the grain race from Australia eight times in succession.

EILIANUS

The British steam coaster *Eilianus*, of Liverpool, lies wrecked under the cliffs at the appropriately named Welcombe Mouth, just north of the Cornish/Devonian border. Bound from Le Havre to Briton Ferry with 800 tons of scrap, she went ashore in dense fog at 12.15 am on 16 June 1936. The crew of eleven, one clad only in his singlet, took to the ship's boat and drifted around in driving mist until daylight when they were able to land at Marsland Mouth. Within 100 yards of the *Eilianus* was the wrecked British coaster *Cambalu*, which had run into Welcombe Mouth three years earlier.

The *Eilianus* was built in Holland in 1917 as the *Wyke Regis*. Her registered tonnage was 333 and her engines developed 112 hp. At the time of her loss she was owned by Mr F. L. Thomas, of Amlwch.

BESSEMER CITY

The sickly stench of fuel oil blowing in over St Ives on the morning of 2 November 1936 was the first indication to many of the townsfolk that there had been a wreck. The victim was the American steamer *Bessemer City,* of New York, bound for London from the USA via Liverpool—with a general cargo, which had gone ashore at Pen Enys Point, about two miles to the west. The St Ives lifeboat had taken off her crew of thirty-three during the night in a strong NNE breeze with a rough sea. In the photo, the *Bessemer City,* already broken in three parts, is being pounded by a northerly swell watched by scores of people lining the edge of Trevalgan Cliffs. Much of her cargo of tinned peaches and salmon found its way into local homes; the author knew of one supply which lasted until well after World War II.

Launched by the Chichasaw Shipbuilding Co in 1921, the *Bessemer City* had a gross tonnage of 5,687, and was 424 ft in length, with a beam of 56 ft.

82

The Elders & Fyffes liner *Manzes,* outward bound from Dartmouth, steams past the *English Trader,* of London, wrecked on the Checkstone Ledge under Dartmouth Castle. She ran onto the rocks early in the morning of 23 January 1937 after she had suffered a steering gear failure when entering the port for bunkers with a cargo of grain from the Argentine. An attempt by the destroyer, HMS *Witch,* and three tugs to tow her off failed, and next day when a SSE gale blew up the Brixham lifeboat had to take off fifty-two crew and salvage personnel. The *English Trader* was refloated on 22 February after her bow section had been cut away and left on the rocks.

After a new bulkhead had been fitted at Dartmouth, she was towed stern-first to Southampton for further repairs before a new bow was built on at a shipyard on the north-east coast. Owned by the Trader Navigation Co, the *English Trader* was built in 1934 as the *Arctees* by the Furness Shipbuilding Co at Haverton Hill-on-Tees. Her gross tonnage was 3,953 and her overall length 374 ft, with a beam of 57 ft. Her end came in October 1941 when she was driven ashore on Hammond Knoll.

WHITE LADY

The seventy-four holiday makers who boarded the Torquay pleasure steamer
White Lady early in the afternoon of Tuesday, 15 June 1937, settled down to enjoy
a quiet trip that would take them across Torbay, past Berry Head, Mansands,
Scabbacombe Sands and up the River Dart as far as Dittisham. However, just off
the entrance to the Dart, the trip came to a juddering halt when the *White Lady*
ran onto a reef of rocks inside the Mew Stone. Luckily the sea was calm and other
pleasure boats in the vicinity were able to take off all the passengers. The *White
Lady*, owned by Mr W. J. Peters of Torquay, is seen here with the Mew Stone
behind her. The clearly defined high-water mark on the rock shows that the tide
was low at the time. The *White Lady* floated off on the evening tide, having suffered
only minor damage.

A mile NW of St Just, in Cornwall, between Botallack Head and Kenidjack Castle, in an area dominated by the ruins of abandoned mine workings, lie the remains of the Italian steamer *Aida Lauro* of Naples. She ran ashore in thick fog in the early hours of 1 July 1937, while bound from West Africa to Hull, via Liverpool. Her cargo included peanuts, which were washed up in large quantities on the beaches at St Ives and eagerly collected and eaten by the youngsters of the borough. The St Ives lifeboat took off fifteen of the crew, the remainder coming ashore in the ship's boats. The *Aida Lauro* broke her back two days later and very rapidly went to pieces.

Built at Stockton in 1923 as the *Radnor* by the Richardson Shipbuilding & Dock Co, she was later renamed *Treharris* and in the same year as she was lost was sold to Alfredo Lauro, of Naples, who gave her her final name. Her gross tonnage was 4,538 and she had a length of 413 ft, with a beam of 52 ft.

ALBA

Just after 7 pm on 31 January 1938 the St Ives lifeboat *Caroline Parsons* was launched into the teeth of a strong northerly gale after a ship had been reported aground on nearby Porthmeor beach. Hundreds of people who rushed down to the Island, from where the lights of the stricken ship could be seen, were eye witnesses to the dramatic scenes that were to follow. The lifeboat came under the lee of the ship, the Panamanian-registered steamer *Alba*, bound from Barry to Civita Vecchia with coal and took off her crew of twenty-three. By now, however, the tide was quickly ebbing and while getting clear of the *Alba* the lifeboat was overturned by a huge sea and thrown up onto the rocks below the Island. Many brave acts were carried out by policemen, members of the LSA and other townsfolk that night as they risked their lives by wading into the crashing surf, but despite their gallantry five of the crew of the *Alba* were drowned.

In the photograph, taken on the following morning, the *Caroline Parsons* can be seen lying on the rocks a total loss, while behind her the *Alba* has already lost her funnel. The *Alba* of 2,310 tons gross and built by the Detroit Shipbuilding Co as the *Cayuga* in 1920, quickly broke up, although much of her cargo was burned in the grates of local homes.

TARASCON

The French trawler *Tarascon,* of Boulogne, lies tightly wedged between the rocks under the near-vertical cliffs of Steeple Cove, about one mile WNW of Bolt Head, near Salcombe, where she ran aground at 5 am on 23 March 1938. Five of the trawler's crew of twenty rowed to Soar Mill Cove where they landed safely despite a heavy ground swell, and were then spotted by a coastguard. Salcombe lifeboat was called out and found the remaining crew members huddled at the foot of the cliffs, soaked through and cold. The lifeboat was unable to get very close so she fired a line over to the shipwrecked crew and dragged them, one by one, through the sea to the lifeboat. Almost miraculously, the trawler was refloated sometime later on a very high tide, using block and tackle fixed to two rocks astern of the vessel. A large motorboat helped to tow her off and she was then handed over to a tug for towing to Plymouth.

The deep-sea tug *Empire Harry,* towing two laden lighters, was caught by a sw gale in Bigbury Bay, South Devon, on 6 June 1945 and blown ashore at Beacon Point between Hope Cove and Thurlestone. The tug's crew of nineteen were taken off by the Salcombe lifeboat, but the tug and the lighters became total losses and their wreckage is today strewn under the cliff walk from Hope Cove to Warren Point.

The *Empire Harry,* built at Goole in 1943 by the Goole Shipbuilding & Repair Co Ltd, was owned by the Ministry of War Transport and managed by the United Towing Co Ltd. She was 136 ft long with a beam of 30 ft and had a gross tonnage of 479. Her engine developed 197 hp. An interesting point to note in the photograph is the gun platform situated abaft the mainmast, a reminder that the war in Europe had only recently ended.

SAND RUNNER

Early holiday-makers are viewing with interest a ship with the rather appropriate name of *Sand Runner*, which had come ashore on Porthmeor Beach, St Ives, during a dense fog. The date was 31 May 1950, and the casualty had been inward bound to Hayle with a cargo of coal from Barry. The St Ives LSA fired a line over the ship but the crew elected to stay aboard until she refloated on the next tide.

The *Sand Runner*, registered at Goole, had been built at Thorn in 1943 by R. Dunstan, as one of a small class of wartime-built, shallow-draught vessels. Of only 313 tons gross, she had a length of 141 ft and a breadth of 22 ft. She continued trading until 1967 when she was broken up at Northam, Southampton.

LIBERTY

Often it is a race between the sea and the salvors when a wreck is sold by the insurers as a total constructive loss. In the case of the Liberian steamer *Liberty*, the wreckage was hauled up the cliff by winch to be sold as scrap. In this photograph, taken seven months after the steamer had run aground, demolition work is well in hand. The salvage men have cut two gaping holes through the ship's hull, primarily to reduce the impact of waves breaking on the wreck.

The *Liberty* went ashore under Pendeen lighthouse in a NW gale on 17 January 1952, after failing to keep up a sufficient head of steam while bound from Newport to La Goulette in ballast. The St Just LSA rescued twenty-two of the crew during the night, but in the morning thirteen nervous Lascars, who had hidden themselves away, were also brought ashore in the breeches buoy.

Built by Palmers at Hebburn-on-Tyne in 1919 as the *Cairdhu*, she was renamed *Styrmion* in 1927 and later, *Liberty*. Her gross tonnage was 5,250, length 399 ft, breadth 52 ft and depth 28 ft.

The minesweeper HMS *Wave* is here seen being battered by huge seas whipped up by a NE gale as she lies aground near Pedn-Olva rocks after her anchor cable had parted in St Ives Bay at 5 am on 30 September 1952. As a precautionary measure, sixty-one members of her crew of ninety-two were brought ashore by breeches buoy, soaked and smothered in fuel oil as were many of the members of the St Ives LSA who had set up their apparatus on Westcott's Quay. After the tide receded, the minesweeper was seen to be impaled on the rocks, with holes in her engine and boiler rooms. Local fishermen shook their heads, saying that she would never get off, but she was successfully refloated on 2 October with the aid of the boom defence ship *Barbastel* after a barrage balloon had been placed in a holed fuel tank and inflated to provide her with additional buoyancy. Temporary repairs were carried out alongside Smeatons Pier, and on 7 October she was towed to Plymouth by the tug *Freebooter*.

A minesweeper of the 'Algerine' class, the *Wave* was built at Lobnitz in 1944 and was eventually broken up at Gateshead in 1962.

VENUS

With her bows almost out of the water, the Norwegian cruise liner *Venus*, of Bergen, makes a striking sight as she sits on the rocks of Dead Man's Bay in Plymouth Sound. She arrived at Plymouth on 22 March 1955 from Madeira and Teneriffe, and after disembarking 250 passengers anchored inside the breakwater to take on stores. During the night the wind veered to the south-west and increased to gale force, and early on the following morning she dragged her anchors and was blown ashore. Coastguards fired a line over her, but those of the 150 crew who were not needed aboard were sent ashore in the ship's boats. After a number of unsuccessful attempts, the *Venus* was eventually towed off on the morning tide on 26 March and taken to Devonport Dockyard for temporary repairs.

After major repairs in Holland she continued cruising until 1968, when she was broken up for scrap. Owned by the Bergenske Steamship Co Ltd, she was built at Elsinore in 1931 with a gross tonnage of 5,407, a length of 398 ft and a beam of 54 ft. She was a twin-screw vessel with four-cycle, 10-cylinder diesels of 9,550 bhp.

VERT PRAIRIAL
(facing page, left)

Just after daylight on Wednesday, 14 March 1956, Mr Leslie Treweren of Porthcurno set out to collect driftwood. At the water's edge he noticed a very strong smell of oil and then he saw a smashed-up lifeboat which had been washed ashore. On the way back up the cliff to warn the coastguards, he spotted the bows of a trawler under Pedn-Men-an-mere Point. The rescue services, which had been alerted several hours earlier after a weak distress call had been picked up, rushed to the scene but there was no sign of any survivors.

The wreck proved to be that of the French trawler *Vert Prairial*, of Dieppe. As the tide receded she could be seen lying on her port side almost totally surrounded by rocks. Her loss was a mystery as the night had been clear with only a moderate wind, and the heavy swell which had been breaking on the rocks could have been heard some distance out to sea. The 125 ft-long trawler had been bound from Brixham to the Trevose fishing grounds with a crew of seventeen. She was built at Sorel in Canada in 1948, and was of 270 tons gross.

YEWCROFT
(below right)

On the evening of Sunday, 8 July 1956, a dense fog covered the whole of West Cornwall. A local resident walking along the cliffs above the beach at Perranuthnoe heard the noise of a ship's engines, and then to his amazement spotted a ship running in towards the coast. He shouted in an attempt to warn her off, but minutes later the ship grounded near Stackhouse Cove, on the St Michaels Mount side of Cudden Point. Penlee lifeboat was called out, but on the way to the wreck stranded herself on rocks near the Mount for a short time. The casualty was the Glasgow-registered coastal steamer *Yewcroft*, bound from London to Bristol with cement. About two hours after she stranded, she suddenly broke her back as the ebbing tide left her bows and stern perched on rocks. Ten of her crew then jumped into the lifeboat, while the remaining member came ashore in the breeches buoy operated by Porthleven LSA team.

The *Yewcroft*, of 827 tons gross and owned by John Stewart & Co, was built at Bowling in 1929 by Scott & Sons. She had a length of 195 ft, a beam of 31 ft, and her engine developed 90 hp. In the photograph, Cudden Point stands out towards the horizon, while the *Yewcroft* lies abandoned, her fate sealed by her broken back.

NAZARENE

The camera has recorded the sad sight of the *Nazarene,* one of the last of the once large fleet of St Ives fishing luggers, stranded on Pedn-e-Vounder beach, near Porthcurnow. Within a few hours she was to be pounded to pieces by a heavy ground sea coming in on the flood tide. She had gone ashore in dense fog at 3 am on Saturday, 21 September 1957, when returning to Newlyn from the fishing grounds with her catch of 120 stone of pilchards. Her skipper, J. F. Toman, and his crew of four stayed aboard until the tide receded and at daylight climbed the cliffs and then walked to the village of Treen where the sub-postmaster telephoned the coastguards. The crew spent the morning lightening their boat by pulling nets, gear and the catch ashore, and on the following Monday and Tuesday were joined by over sixty fishermen from St Ives and Mounts Bay who hauled fishing gear worth over £1,000 from the beach to the top of the steep cliffs.

The *Nazarene* was built by Bawden, at Porthleven, in 1900 as a double-ended pilchard boat. When launched, she had a length of 32 ft, but in 1920 she was modified at St Ives by H. Trevorrow & Son, and her length increased to 45 ft. At the same time, a square stern and a new keel were fitted.

94

The coastal tanker *Allegrity,* of London, lies capsized on the rocks under the cliffs at Caerhays, near the Dodman, in South Cornwall. Bound from Le Havre to the Mersey with 700 tons of lubricating oil, she had first struck Grebe Point, near Porthscatho, at 5 am on 13 December 1961 during a south-west gale, came off, and then drifted nine miles across Veryan Bay. In a dramatic rescue, Falmouth lifeboat took off her crew of fourteen, two lifeboatmen having to board the tanker to help one man who was suffering from shock.

Owned by F. T. Everard & Co, the *Allegrity* had been built by the Grangemouth Shipbuilding Co in 1945 as the *Empire Tavistock,* being renamed *Sobat* in 1946 and *Allegrity* in 1951. Of 798 tons gross, she was 193 ft in length, with a breadth of 31 ft and a depth of 14 ft.

On 3 November 1962 there occurred a tragedy and at the same time probably the most remarkable sea rescue ever carried out in Devon or Cornwall. The French trawler, *Jeanne Gougy*, of Dieppe, of 273 tons gross and built in 1948, ran aground on the northern side of Dr Syntax's Head at Land's End during a heavy rain squall at about 5 am when homeward bound from the Irish fishing grounds with a crew of eighteen. Her distress flares brought out the life-saving teams and the Sennen Cove lifeboat but, to their horror, the hopeful rescuers saw the trawler roll over on to her port side and become submerged under hundreds of tons of water as huge seas swept over her. All hope had been given up, but as the tide receded at midday a movement was seen in the trawler's wheelhouse. After two rocket lines had been fired over the ship the survivor inside the wheelhouse managed to pull the breeches buoy aboard. Then to the amazement of the hundreds of onlookers on the cliffs, four more survivors rushed out of the forecastle and were pulled ashore in the breeches buoy. The crew member in the wheelhouse was too weak to help himself, so an airman was lowered on a rope from a helicopter and pulled him up to safety. The airman then returned, and after some time in the wheelhouse, reappeared with another member of the crew. In all, eleven men, including the master, lost their lives in the wreck. In the photograph, salvage work is in progress after the wreck had been sold to a scrap dealer for £250.

GREEN RANGER

The Admiralty tanker *Green Ranger,* of 3,313 tons gross, lies a total wreck with her back broken below the 400 ft high cliffs at Longpeak, between Bude and Hartland, in North Cornwall. Caught in a force 10 northerly gale on the afternoon of 17 November 1962, she was blown ashore at 6 pm after the tug *Caswell* had slipped the tow rope when towing the tanker from Plymouth to Cardiff for a refit. Hartland LSA were quickly on the scene but could not reach the ship with their rockets because the hurricane-force winds were blowing dead onshore. They therefore waited until the tide ebbed and then climbed down the near-vertical cliffs with their gear – no mean feat, as can be seen from the photograph. They made contact with their first rocket fired from the foot of the cliffs and brought the towing crew of seven ashore in the breeches buoy. This magnificent rescue earned the Hartland team the Ministry of Transport's shield for the best wreck service of the year. The coxwain of the Appledore lifeboat was awarded the silver medal of the RNLI and each of the crew a record of thanks inscribed on vellum for their gallantry in manoeuvring their boat close to the tanker and remaining there for fifteen minutes in extreme danger while, with the aid of their searchlight and loud-hailer, they tried unsuccessfully to attract the attention of the men on the *Green Ranger* who had taken refuge below decks.

The tanker, which was built at Dundee in 1942 by the Caledon Shipbuilding & Engineering Co, had a length of 340 ft and a beam of 48·3 ft.

Salvage men, standing on her deck, view with apprehension the huge column of spray sent up as a wave crashes against the side of the motor coaster *Alacrity* stranded in Portheras Cove, half a mile east of Pendeen Watch. Shortly afterwards they tried to row ashore in their dinghy, but this overturned in the surf and they had to swim to the beach. The *Alacrity* had gone ashore in thick fog at 6.30 am on the previous day, Friday 13 September 1963, while bound from Swansea to Brussels with 600 tons of anthracite dust for power-station use. No distress call was put out until noon, but after the local LSA team arrived on the scene the crew rowed ashore in one of the ship's boats. On 22 September the *Alacrity* was abandoned as a constructive total loss and in the following months was dismantled by a salvage firm who hauled her remains up the cliff by winch.

Built in 1940 by the Goole Shipbuilding Co, the *Alacrity* was owned by the well known London firm of F. T. Everard & Co. She was 554 tons gross and had a length of 169 ft, with a beam of 28 ft.

Less than eighteen months after the loss of the *Jeanne Gougy* another trawler was totally wrecked only 200 yards away under the precipitous cliffs of Gamper Cove, on the Sennen Cove side of Dr Syntax's Head. The victim this time was the Belgian trawler *Victoire Rogers*, of Ostend, which went aground in thick misty weather at 4 am on 24 March 1964. The crew, who had been on deck preparing the nets, sent out an SOS and guided the Sennen Cove lifeboat to the scene by red lights and a fire made from blankets and beds. Despite the heavy seas that were breaking on the rocks surrounding the trawler, the lifeboat made a quick run in, snatched off four of the crew, and then returned again to rescue the skipper who had a broken arm. The lifeboat touched bottom several times, but luckily no damage was suffered and the crew of the *Victoire Rogers* were landed at Newlyn at 6.15 that morning.

Despite the undamaged appearance of the trawler in the photograph, she was already holed below the waterline and had to be abandoned. A salvage company later cut a hole in her side and removed her engine, and then cut up the remainder of the ship piecemeal for scrap.

TORREY CANYON

This could almost be an aerial photograph of a tanker under way, but closer examinations shows that the sea around her is covered with thick black oil. She is the giant and infamous Liberian *Torrey Canyon* which was wrecked on the Seven Stones Reef, between the Land's End and the Scilly Isles, on 18 March 1967 while bound from the Persian Gulf to Milford Haven with 120,000 tons of oil. Off her starboard bow, and dwarfed by her huge size, lies the St Mary's lifeboat, and in the right background the sea can be seen breaking over one of the rocks of the reef. A final attempt was made to tow her off on the highest spring tide on 26 March, but she suddenly broke in three parts and the oil trickle now became a gusher. Oil was swept ashore from Trevose Head to the Lizard, in places 18in deep, and thousands of dead and oiled seabirds were washed ashore. Pollution became so severe that the government decided to bomb her, and during the next two days she was bombarded by 1,000 lb bombs, hundreds of gallons of kerosene, and a number of napalm bombs. Most of the remaining oil aboard burned but for weeks afterwards a gigantic oil clearing operation took place all around the coasts of Cornwall, costing over £1,600,000.

Built at Newport News, Virginia, in 1965, the *Torrey Canyon* had a length of 974 ft and a deadweight tonnage of 118,285.

The stranding of the tug *Fusee II* at Bude on 23 April 1969 evoked memories among the older residents of the many sailing ships which had been wrecked when navigating the dangerous entrance to this once busy port. The tug, bound from her home port of Swansea to Plymouth, developed engine trouble in a force eight NW gale and her skipper decided to beach her. She came ashore on Crooklets Beach before daylight, with lights flashing and an SOS being sounded on her siren. This brought local people rushing to the scene just in time to see her five-man crew rowing ashore in a dinghy. During the next tide the tug was driven across the beach and ended up under the cliffs near the Bude bathing pool. Two local men acquired the salvage rights and succeeded in refloating the tug on the spring tide of 29 April.

Behind the tug in the photograph can be seen the narrow entrance to Bude Haven flanked by the breakwater and the Chapel Rock, so named because prior to the sixteenth century a small chapel dedicated to St Michael stood on this unlikely spot. On the headland, known as Compass Point, stands the weather-beaten octagonal tower built in 1830 and used as a coastguard look-out.

HEMSLEY I

On 10 May 1969 the British steam tanker *Hemsley I*, at that time the oldest trading vessel flying the 'red duster', left the Mersey on her last voyage, bound for a breakers' yard in Antwerp. She never reached her destination because, at 1.54 am on 12 May, she was sending a radio message reporting that she was ashore in dense fog under the Lizard lighthouse. The Coverack and Lizard lifeboats were launched and coastguards searched the cliffs, but it was not until 5.30 am, after one of her crew had climbed the cliffs and phoned the police, that she was located on the North Cornish coast in Fox Cove, near Padstow. The *Hemsley I* is seen here almost surrounded by the rocks which were to be her final resting place.

She was built by the Tyne Iron Shipbuilding Co Ltd at Newcastle in 1916 as the *Scotol* for the Admiralty, at a time when the Royal Navy was changing over from coal to oil-firing. Her design included a clear area amidships to facilitate oiling warships while under way, which accounts for the unusual position of her bridge. Since 1948 she had been owned by Hemsley Bell Ltd and had been used for bunkering services.

LENIE

Holiday-makers line the cliffs on the eastern side of Soar Mill Cove, in South Devon, on 20 July 1972 where the Dutch motor coaster *Lenie* lies aground only one mile westward along the coast from where the *Amelie Suzanne* had been lost three months earlier. The *Lenie* had run ashore at 3.30 am that morning in dense fog while bound from Par to Rotterdam with a cargo of china clay. Salcombe life-boat hurried to the scene but as the sea was dead calm the crew of eight and the captain's wife and two children preferred to remain aboard the stranded ship. The *Lenie* refloated at high water, just before 1.30 pm, with the assistance of the lifeboat, seen alongside the stern of the coaster in the photograph. The large rock in the right background is the Ham Stone and just to the left of this, almost hidden in the fog, is the ocean-going tug *Welshman* which had put out from Brixham in case her assistance was needed.

The *Lenie*, registered at Steendam, was built at Haugesund in 1962 with a gross tonnage of 400 and a length of 160 ft.

LA VARENNE

Directly under the First and Last House at Land's End is a little inlet known locally as Dollar Cove, probably named after some long-forgotten wreck. The wooden French trawler *La Varenne,* of Cherbourg, is seen here trapped right up under the granite columns of the cove where she ran aground in the early hours of 7 September 1972. Sennen lifeboat was launched after the owner's wife at nearby Penwith House had spotted the distress flares sent up from the stricken ship. Despite the heavy swell that was running, all eight members of the crew were safely taken off by the lifeboat, but the *La Varenne,* of 118 tons gross and built at Concarneau in 1958, became a total wreck.

NEFELI

By a remarkable coincidence, less than two months after the wreck of the *La Varenne* and while she was still being dismantled by a salvage firm, the Cypriot motor vessel *Nefeli* drove ashore in Dollar Cove right on top of the *La Varenne*. She had earlier lost her rudder after striking the Kettles Bottom in dense fog when a fire had put her radar out of action. Bound from Garston to Antwerp in ballast, she stranded just after 3 am on 5 November 1972. All eleven of the crew were rescued by the LSA, and although at first there were high hopes that she could be refloated, by 20 November she had broken completely in two and rapidly went to pieces.

The *Nefeli* was no stranger to Cornwall as for many years after her launching at Ardrossan in 1957 for the Queenship Navigation Co, she had loaded stone at Newlyn. She had been sold to the Nefeli Shipping Co of Cyprus only two months before her loss. The *Nefeli* is seen here when photographed during a brief clearance in the fog a few hours after she had been wrecked. Beyond her lies the magnificent rock islet of the Armed Knight.

SUGGESTIONS FOR FURTHER READING

Richard Larn and Clive Carter: *Cornish Shipwrecks Vol 1 The South Coast*, David & Charles, 1969.

Clive Carter: *Cornish Shipwrecks Vol 2 The North Coast*, David & Charles, 1970.

Richard Larn: *Cornish Shipwrecks Vol 3 The Isles of Scilly*, David & Charles, 1971.

Richard Larn: *Devon Shipwrecks*, David & Charles, 1974.

These four volumes each record details of some hundreds of shipwrecks and are illustrated by numerous photographs and wreck location charts.

Crispin Gill, Frank Booker and Tony Soper: *The Wreck of the Torrey Canyon*, David & Charles, 1967. A factual record of the stranding of the 118,000 ton super-tanker, supported by many photographs.

John Arlott (in collaboration with Rex Cowan and Frank Gibson): *Island Camera*. The Isles of Scilly in the Photography of the Gibson Family. David & Charles, 1972. A unique pictorial record of the Isles of Scilly, including a number of photographs of ships and shipwreck.

Michael Bouquet: *Westcountry Sail*. Merchant Shipping 1840–1960. David & Charles, 1971. A pictorial record of Westcountry rigs, shipyards and harbours.

Clive Carter: *The Blizzard of '91*, David & Charles, 1971. A dramatic account of the unprecedented blizzard which swept the Westcountry in March 1891, in the course of which 63 ships foundered between the Goodwins and the Isles of Scilly.

Cyril Noall and Grahame Farr: *Wreck and Rescue Round the Cornish Coast* Vol 1, The Story of the North Coast Lifeboats.

Vol 2, The Story of the Land's End Lifeboats.

Vol 3, The Story of the South Coast Lifeboats.

D. Bradford Barton, 1964, 1965, 1965 respectively.

Grahame Farr: *Wreck and Rescue on the Coast of Devon*. The Story of the South Devon Lifeboats. D. Bradford Barton, 1968.

Grahame Farr: *Wreck and Rescue in the Bristol Channel*. The Story of the English Lifeboats. D. Bradford Barton, 1966.

These five volumes give the story of each of the lifeboat stations, past and present, around the coast of the South West. Details of many shipwrecks are given and the volumes include a number of photographs of lifeboats and shipwrecks.

ACKNOWLEDGEMENTS

Over the years that I have been collecting shipwreck photographs, I have made many acquaintances and friendships with people who have helped in the search for new photographs, identification of unknown wreck photos, and the compilation of wreck details. In particular, I have enjoyed many years of interchange of information with Grahame Farr, the lifeboat historian of Portishead, Bristol; Edward Blight of Manchester, an expert on Bude wrecks and shipping; John Davies, Truro; Clive Carter, Sancreed; Percy Barnes, Carbis Bay; and the late Richard Gillis of Newquay.

I should like to convey my grateful thanks to fellow World Ship Society members, G. H. Somner, J. J. Colledge, L. Gray, and the Rev D. Ridley Chesterton, who have provided an invaluable service from the Society's central record in tracing the history and fates of many of the ships mentioned and correcting some information already published; Richard Larne, St Austell, for photographs and information from his extensive files; K. R. Mason, shipping editor and T. M. Dinan of Lloyds, for much useful information; Inspector L. Torne of HM Coastguard, St Ives; George Ransome, Manchester; David Murch of Salcombe; HM Customs and Excise, Library Museum and Records.

I am also indebted to the Shipwrecked Mariners' Society; L. W. Moore, Chairman, Port of Lowestoft Research Society, for information on Lowestoft-registered wrecks; Head of Naval Historical Library, Ministry of Defence; General Register of Shipping and Seamen, Cardiff; Eddie Murt, St Ives; John Chase, Lyme Regis; Michael Dowdell of Torquay Public Library; the Royal National Lifeboat Institution; Percy Jarvis, Hope Cove; John Horsley, Curator of Brixham Museum; Curator and Staff of Ilfracombe Museum; Commander Burns and Staff of Plymouth Central Library; H. L. Douch, Curator, and R. Penhallurick of the Royal Institution of Cornwall, Truro; Bob Sadler, proprietor of the *Kingsbridge Times*; and, lastly, to John Davies again for giving up some of his valuable time in the search for new wreck photographs.

Finally, my sincere thanks to Terry Pinder of Paignton for his photographic work and help; my mother for help in reading through newspaper files, and to my wife for many hours of typing and for enduring my 'wrecking' escapades.

J.J.B.

Galmpton, Devon.

SOURCES OF ILLUSTRATIONS

Whenever possible, acknowledgement has been made to the individual or institution from which the illustration originated, but with photographs acquired from many sources over two decades it was not possible in some cases to trace their origin with certainty. These have, therefore, been included under the general heading of the Author's Collection. The figures refer to page numbers.

All other illustrations are from the Author's Collection or from photographs taken by the author.

INDEX OF WRECK ILLUSTRATIONS